WordPress Mobile Applications with PhoneGap

A straightforward, example-based guide to leveraging
your web development skills to build mobile applications
using WordPress, jQuery, jQuery Mobile, and PhoneGap

Yuxian Eugene Liang

BIRMINGHAM - MUMBAI

WordPress Mobile Applications with PhoneGap

First published: November 2012

Production Reference: 1161112

Published by Packt Publishing Ltd.
Livery Place
35 Livery Street
Birmingham B3 2PB, UK.

ISBN 978-1-84951-986-1

www.packtpub.com

Cover Image by John M. Quick (john.m.quick@gmail.com)

Credits

Author
Yuxian Eugene Liang

Reviewers
Ken Cenerelli

Adam D. Scott

Kerri Shotts

Acquisition Editor
Usha Iyer

Commissioning Editors
Maria D'souza

Llewellyn Rozario

Technical Editor
Nitee Shetty

Copy Editors
Brandt D'Mello

Insiya Morbiwala

Aditya Nair

Project Coordinator
Shraddha Bagadia

Proofreader
Aaron Nash

Indexer
Tejal Soni

Production Coordinator
Melwyn D'sa

Cover Work
Melwyn D'sa

About the Author

Yuxian Eugene Liang is a researcher, author, web developer, and business developer. He enjoys solving difficult problems creatively by implementing web applications using Python/Django/Tornado and JavaScript/jQuery/Node.js. He also enjoys doing research related to the areas of social network analysis, social computing, recommendation algorithms, link analysis, data visualization, data mining, information retrieval, business intelligence, and intelligent user interfaces. He previously authored *JavaScript Testing Beginner's Guide, Packt Publishing*. Find him at http://www.liangeugene.com. Support for this book can also be found at http://wordpressphonegap.liangeugene.com.

I am grateful for this opportunity and I certainly want to thank the folks at Packt Publishing, Shraddha Bagadia, Manali Mehta, Maria D'souza, Ninad Vedak, and Namita Nair, who collaborated with me on this book.

Special thanks to Professor Daphne Yuan Soe-Tsyr, Professor Tsai-Yen Li, and Professor Pailin Chen of National Cheng Chi University (NCCU, Taipei Taiwan) for providing me with timely and practical advice on how to do great research and how to deal with life.

To the good people of Service Science Research Centre, Intelligent Media Lab, and the research team of the Flood and Fire research project of NCCU, thank you for helping me out when I needed it most.

I also want to thank Charlene Hsiao, YC. I, and Michelle Yuan for helping me out when both of my hands are down, literally.

Last but not least, my family members and friends for their continued support.

About the Reviewers

Ken Cenerelli is a Senior Software Developer who specializes in designing and creating effective solutions for both the Web and desktop environments. With over 11 years of experience in software design, development, and support, he has engineered strong, data-driven web applications using the Microsoft .NET framework for large and small companies throughout North America. Ken also works with mobile technologies and has built apps for both Windows Phone 7 and the Android OS. In the years prior to his career in software development, he was employed with the newspaper industry, holding jobs as a reporter and a newspaper librarian.

He lives in Ontario, Canada with his wife Renée. Visit his developer's blog at kencenerelli.wordpress.com to see what he is currently exploring, and to learn more about him, you can also follow him on Twitter at @KenCenerelli.

Adam D. Scott is a designer, frontend developer, husband, and father living in Connecticut. He has been a dedicated educator for six years, focusing on web technologies with project-based outcomes. He writes about the intersection of design, technology, and learning at adamdscott.com.

He is the author of the book, *WordPress for Education, Packt Publishing*.

I would like to thank those at Packt Publishing for their dedication to documenting and promoting open source software, and the WordPress community for their continual development of an incredible publishing platform.

Kerri Shotts is an IT Consultant specializing in mobile application development and website design. She can be found most days working from her home near Saint Louis, Missouri. She loves to read and write books and music, enjoys working with her aquariums, and is in love with all things Apple. She is the author of *PhoneGap Hotshot, Packt Publishing*.

I'd like to thank Packt Publishing for this opportunity. I'd also like to thank my family for supporting me in fulfilling my dreams, and my God for giving me the talent and ability.

www.PacktPub.com

Support files, eBooks, discount offers and more

You might want to visit www.PacktPub.com for support files and downloads related to your book.

Did you know that Packt offers eBook versions of every book published, with PDF and ePub files available? You can upgrade to the eBook version at www.PacktPub.com and as a print book customer, you are entitled to a discount on the eBook copy. Get in touch with us at service@packtpub.com for more details.

At www.PacktPub.com, you can also read a collection of free technical articles, sign up for a range of free newsletters and receive exclusive discounts and offers on Packt books and eBooks.

http://PacktLib.PacktPub.com

Do you need instant solutions to your IT questions? PacktLib is Packt's online digital book library. Here, you can access, read and search across Packt's entire library of books.

Why Subscribe?

- Fully searchable across every book published by Packt
- Copy and paste, print and bookmark content
- On demand and accessible via web browser

Free Access for Packt account holders

If you have an account with Packt at www.PacktPub.com, you can use this to access PacktLib today and view nine entirely free books. Simply use your login credentials for immediate access.

Table of Contents

Preface

If you have picked up this book, there is a good chance that you are interested in combining WordPress with PhoneGap and building some really cool mobile applications. While it may not be obvious, WordPress can be used in conjunction with PhoneGap to create native mobile apps, with a powerful backend content management system (CMS) provided by WordPress.

This book shows you how to combine WordPress and PhoneGap so that you can create native mobile apps with minimal coding.

A 30,000-feet overview of this book

How can we use WordPress together with PhoneGap? It turns out that this is possible through the use of WordPress's Application Programming Interface (API). For starters, consider how popular websites such as Facebook, Twitter, and Google allow third-party programmers to extend their website's core functionalities via APIs; third-party developers create mashups or build new applications through two basic requests, namely the GET and POST requests. In this book, you will also learn how to extend your WordPress site's capabilities over to mobile applications.

What this book covers

Chapter 1, *WordPress Overview and Installation*, walks you through a high-level overview of WordPress, from getting it up and running, to its key features such as plugins and themes.

Chapter 2, *Adding Geographical Capabilities via the GeoPlaces Theme*, talks about creating a location-based directory via the GeoPlaces theme. It covers the setting up and addition of sample geographic data into your WordPress site.

Chapter 3, Extending WordPress Using JSON-API, covers how to create your very own API that exposes WordPress's functionality with the JSON-API plugin. From here you'll see how you can quickly create a third-party app based on your WordPress site's content and its exposed API.

Chapter 4, Building Mobile Applications Using PhoneGap, walks you through the installation and creation of a PhoneGap application.

Chapter 5, Extending WordPress to the Mobile World, continues and builds upon the concepts learned in *Chapter 4, Building Mobile Applications Using PhoneGap* You will extend your WordPress site to native mobile applications via PhoneGap. You will learn how easy it is to convert a JavaScript application to a PhoneGap application with just a few lines of code.

Chapter 6, Using Open Source Themes, walks you through applying what we have learned from the first five chapters to open source themes. The theme we are using is the Twenty Ten theme.

What you need for this book

You'll need a basic text editor to get started in this book. Instructions for installing MySQL, PHP, WordPress, and so on are provided in this book.

Who this book is for

This book is for people who are interested in building cross-platform, native mobile applications with a minimum effort for coding. You should have at least a beginner's knowledge of JavaScript/jQuery and WordPress. Knowledge of PhoneGap, JSON, and API-related concepts is not required.

Conventions

In this book, you will find a number of styles of text that distinguish between different kinds of information. Here are some examples of these styles, and an explanation of their meaning.

Code words in text are shown as follows: "We will be writing a `readSinglePost()` function."

A block of code is set as follows:

```
<!DOCTYPE HTML>
<html>
```

```
<head>
<title>Hello World</title>
<script type="text/javascript" charset="utf-8"src="cordova-
1.9.0.js"></script>
</head>
<body>
<h1>Hello World</h1>
</body>
</html>
```

When we wish to draw your attention to a particular part of a code block, the relevant lines or items are set in bold:

```
<body>
<h1>Hello World</h1>
<div id="main">
<div id="title"></div>
<div id="contents"></div>
</div>
</body>
```

New terms and **important words** are shown in bold. Words that you see on the screen, in menus or dialog boxes for example, appear in the text like this: "clicking the **Next** button moves you to the next screen".

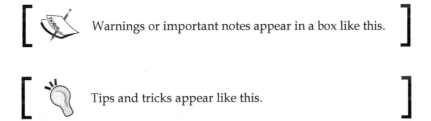

Warnings or important notes appear in a box like this.

Tips and tricks appear like this.

Reader feedback

Feedback from our readers is always welcome. Let us know what you think about this book—what you liked or may have disliked. Reader feedback is important for us to develop titles that you really get the most out of.

To send us general feedback, simply send an e-mail to feedback@packtpub.com, and mention the book title through the subject of your message.

If there is a topic that you have expertise in and you are interested in either writing or contributing to a book, see our author guide on www.packtpub.com/authors.

Customer support

Now that you are the proud owner of a Packt book, we have a number of things to help you to get the most from your purchase.

Downloading the example code

You can download the example code files for all Packt books you have purchased from your account at `http://www.packtpub.com`. If you purchased this book elsewhere, you can visit `http://www.packtpub.com/support` and register to have the files e-mailed directly to you.

Errata

Although we have taken every care to ensure the accuracy of our content, mistakes do happen. If you find a mistake in one of our books — maybe a mistake in the text or the code — we would be grateful if you would report this to us. By doing so, you can save other readers from frustration and help us improve subsequent versions of this book. If you find any errata, please report them by visiting `http://www.packtpub.com/support`, selecting your book, clicking on the **errata submission form** link, and entering the details of your errata. Once your errata are verified, your submission will be accepted and the errata will be uploaded to our website, or added to any list of existing errata, under the Errata section of that title.

Piracy

Piracy of copyright material on the Internet is an ongoing problem across all media. At Packt, we take the protection of our copyright and licenses very seriously. If you come across any illegal copies of our works, in any form, on the Internet, please provide us with the location address or website name immediately so that we can pursue a remedy.

Please contact us at `copyright@packtpub.com` with a link to the suspected pirated material.

We appreciate your help in protecting our authors, and our ability to bring you valuable content.

Questions

You can contact us at `questions@packtpub.com` if you are having a problem with any aspect of the book, and we will do our best to address it.

1
WordPress Overview and Installation

Firstly, welcome to WordPress Mobile Applications with PhoneGap! Before we continue with this book, make sure to go through the *Preamble* section.

Preamble

For a start, why would you be interested in using WordPress together with PhoneGap? I would ask, "Why wouldn't you?" My opinion is that WordPress is among the easiest-to-use content management systems with the required basic functions/features built-in, which includes registration, administration panel, posts management, and so on. More importantly, you can extend it in almost any way you want through the use of plugins and themes. How does this relate to PhoneGap? Using WordPress with PhoneGap means that all forms of common content management issues can be handled using WordPress, while all you need to focus on is to use PhoneGap to serve this content. As simple as that.

Before we begin, make sure your computer is capable of running PHP and MySQL. You should also install phpMyAdmin for easy management of MySQL databases. You should also have access to your web server (local or remote) via shell or FTP, a text editor, FTP client, and a web browser of your choice.

If you do not have a working web server on your computer, you can visit and download the appropriate distributions/packages shown in the next subsections, for your computer.

Mac

Mac OS ships with Apache and PHP. MySQL will have to be compiled to run natively, and this can be cumbersome. If you have limited experience in sysadmin skills, feel free to download and install pre-configured PHP-MySQL packages, such as the following:

- **MAMP**: This can be downloaded and installed from `http://www.mamp.info`
- **XAMPP**: This can be downloaded and installed from `http://www.apachefriends.org/en/xampp.html`

Windows

There are many options for installing and configuring your environment. Some of the options are as follows:

- **XAMPP**: This can be downloaded and installed from `http://www.apachefriends.org/en/xampp.html`
- **WAMP**: This can be downloaded and installed from `http://www.wampserver.com`
- **EasyPHP**: This can be downloaded and installed from `http://www.easyphp.org`

If you are still having issues, please visit `http://codex.WordPress.org/Installing_WordPress#Things_to_Know_Before_Installing_WordPress`.

Downloading the example code

You can download the example code files for all Packt books you have purchased from your account at `http://www.packtpub.com`. If you purchased this book elsewhere, you can visit `http://www.packtpub.com/support` and register to have the files e-mailed directly to you. For the purposes of this book, I'll be developing the application on a local computer; feel free to follow suit by installing the required web server and other related web technologies mentioned earlier in this section.

The famous five minute installation of WordPress

Now, let us quickly install WordPress so we are on the same frequency:

1. Pop over to `http://WordPress.org/download/` and download WordPress in either the `.zip` or `.tar.gz` format. At the time of writing, the latest stable version of WordPress was 3.3.2. Unzip WordPress and place it into a desired location on your local web server.

2. Next, let's create a database for WordPress on your website. For the purposes of this book, I've decided to name my database `wordpress_phonegap`. In my case, I created the database `wordpress_phonegap` using phpMyAdmin:

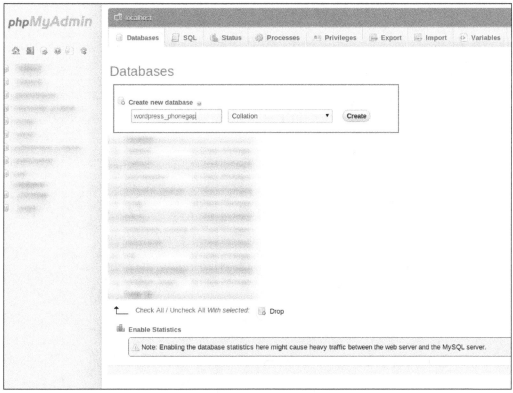

Creating a database using phpMyAdmin

3. Type in `wordpress_phonegap` and click on **Create.**

4. Now, go to the root of your WordPress folder and you should see a file named `wp-config-sample.php`. Open up the file in the text editor of your choice and look for these lines: `define('DB_NAME', 'database_name_here');`, `define('DB_USER' and 'username_here');`, `define('DB_PASSWORD', 'password_here');`. Change `database_name_here`, `username_here`, and `password_here` to the appropriate values and save the file as `wp-config.php`.

5. Now open up your web browser and navigate to the location where you have placed your WordPress installation. In my case, I renamed the WordPress folder to `worpress_phonegap` and I have placed the folder at `http://localhost/public_html`. Hence, this is what I will see when I visit `http://localhost/public_html/WordPress_phonegap`:

Setup page for WordPress

Now enter the information for the **Site Title**, **Username**, **Passwords**, and **Your E-mail** fields. Once done, click on the button **Install WordPress**. For the purposes of this book, I named the site as `WordPress and PhoneGap Mobile Applications` and I am using `admin` as the username.

Once you have successfully installed WordPress, you should see the following on your browser:

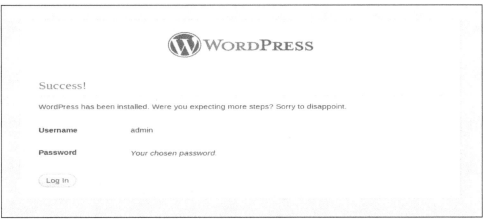

Success message when you have installed WordPress successfully

A five minute introduction to WordPress

WordPress is a free and popular open source **Content Management System (CMS)** that started life as a simple blogging system. It evolved over the years and its look, feel, and capabilities can be easily extended by its themes and plugins.

We will quickly go through the capabilities of WordPress and see how we can leverage on WordPress to build mobile applications of it. The two main capabilities of WordPress that we can leverage on are: themes and plugins.

Themes

Themes in general control the look and feel of any WordPress installation. Going over to http://WordPress.org/extend/themes/, you will see a wide selection of themes that you can download and try for free (most of the time).

For a start, navigate to your WordPress site on your web browser. If you have not made any changes to the site, you should see something like the following on your screen:

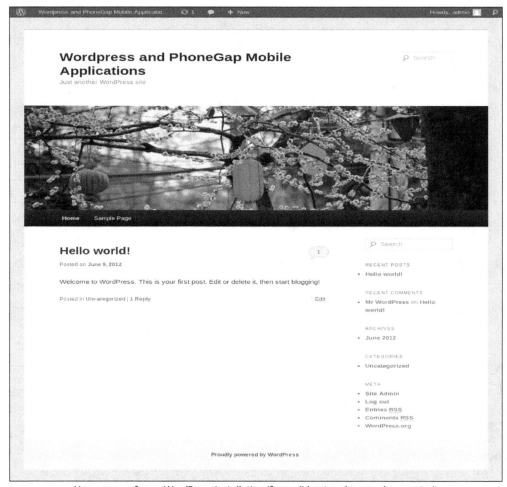

Home page of your WordPress installation if you did not make any changes to it

The earlier screenshot is the default theme of WordPress. Now log in to your WordPress site at `http://localhost/public_html/wordpress_phonegap/wp-admin` and navigate to **Appearance**. You should see that the **Available Themes** option provides you with another theme to play with, called **Twenty Ten**. Click on **Activate** and navigate to your home page again. You should see the following:

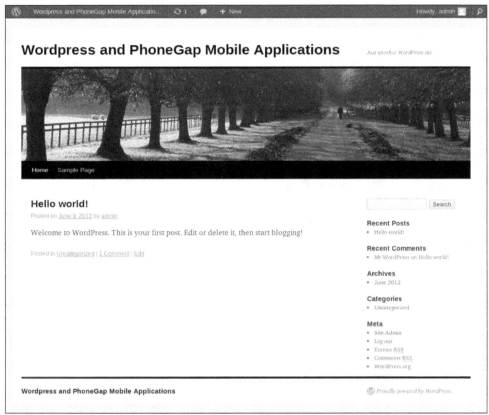

The Twenty Ten theme

The look and feel of your WordPress site is now changed. With a wide variety of themes out there, you can quickly and easily make changes to how your site looks and feels in just a matter of seconds.

Note that we can easily create a mobile website with WordPress by using a mobile theme or themes that support mobile devices. This may be a quick and easy way to create mobile applications out of WordPress, but it does not provide a native interface for the application. Later in this book we will learn about PhoneGap, which is a great way to build native mobile apps using web development techniques. We will be using two themes for this book: one is the GeoPlaces theme that we will be using from *Chapter 3, Extending WordPress Using JSON-API*, to *Chapter 5, Extending WordPress to the Mobile World*; the other theme we will be using is the Twenty Ten theme that comes by default with all WordPress installations. We will be covering the Twenty Ten theme in *Chapter 6, Using Open Source Themes*, of this book.

Plugins

As with all good CMSs, WordPress provides an **Application Programming Interface (API)** that allows developers to quickly and easily extend the functionalities of a WordPress site. Examples of uses of plugins include adding Facebook's popular "**Like**" button to each of your posts and extending the administration side of WordPress, such as user management, and adding in search engine optimization capabilities to your WordPress.

While this book is not about developing plugins for WordPress, it's good to understand the power of WordPress plugins. A good example as to how far plugins can take your WordPress site is WordPress's very own BuddyPress (`http://codex.buddypress.org`) plugin. We will not be making use of BuddyPress in this book, but it's good to see it in action for the purposes of this section:

1. Log in to your WordPress site and navigate to **Plugins** | **Add New**.
2. Search for **BuddyPress**.
3. You can install **BuddyPress** by clicking on **Install Now**, and in no time you will have a working social networking site.

This is the power of WordPress plugins. In this book, we will check out an awesome plugin, called JSON API (`http://WordPress.org/extend/plugins/json-api/`), which can be readily adapted and used for extending our WordPress website.

Summary

By now, you have a working WordPress installation. You should also understand how themes and plugins can be used to extend WordPress. In the next chapter you will see how we can add geographic capabilities to your WordPress site using the GeoPlaces theme.

2
Adding Geographic Capabilities via the GeoPlaces Theme

In this chapter, we'll add geographic capabilities to our WordPress site by leveraging on the GeoPlaces theme. Recall from the previous chapter that we can enhance the capabilities of WordPress through the use of themes and plugins.

For a start, we'll be using a premium theme called GeoPlaces, by Templatic. At the time of writing, a single user license is priced at USD 99 while a developer license is priced at USD 179. Don't worry if you do not wish to purchase or use this theme, as we will be demonstrating the techniques learned in this book on an open source theme called Twenty Ten, in the last chapter of this book.

For the rest of this chapter we will be using the GeoPlaces theme to do the bulk of the heavy lifting of geographic functionalities, since Google Maps are built directly into the GeoPlaces theme.

The major topics we will cover in this chapter are:

- Introduction to the GeoPlaces theme
- Populating the site with sample data from GeoPlaces
- Managing place listings from the frontend side as well as the admin side of the site

Before we move into this chapter officially, you might be wondering where it will lead us. To begin with, since our mobile app's content is dependent on our WordPress site, we need to add basic content (in this case, place listings and other article-like information) to the site.

Introducing the GeoPlaces theme

The GeoPlaces theme (`http://templatic.com/app-themes/geo-places-city-directory-WordPress-theme/`), by Templatic (`http://templatic.com`), is a cool theme that allows you to create and manage a city directory website. For a live demo of the site, visit `http://templatic.com/demos/?theme=geoplaces4`.

An overview of the GeoPlaces theme

The GeoPlaces theme is created as an out-of-the-box solution for city directory websites. It allows end users to submit places and events to your site. Best of all, you can even monetize the site by charging a listing fee. Some of the powerful features include the following:

- Widgetized homepage
- Menu widgets
- Featured events and listings
- Custom fields
- Payment options
- Price packages page view

Let's now move on to the setting up of the theme.

Setting up the GeoPlaces theme

We'll start with the installation of the GeoPlaces theme.

Installation

The steps for installing the GeoPlaces theme are as follows:

1. You will first have to purchase and download your theme (in a zip folder) from Templatic.
2. Unzip the zipped file and place the `GeoPlaces` folder in your `wp-content/themes` folder.
3. Log in to your WordPress site, which we have set up in the first chapter, and activate the theme. Alternatively, you can upload the theme by uploading the theme's zip folder via the admin interface, by going to **Appearance | Install Themes | Upload**.

4. If everything goes well, you should see the following on the navigation bar of your admin page:

5. If you see the previous screenshot in your navigation, than you are ready to move on to the next step.

Populating the site with sample data

After a successful installation of the theme, you can go ahead and play around with the site by creating sample data. GeoPlaces themes come with a nifty function that allows you to populate your site with sample data. Navigate to wp-admin/themes. php and you should see the following:

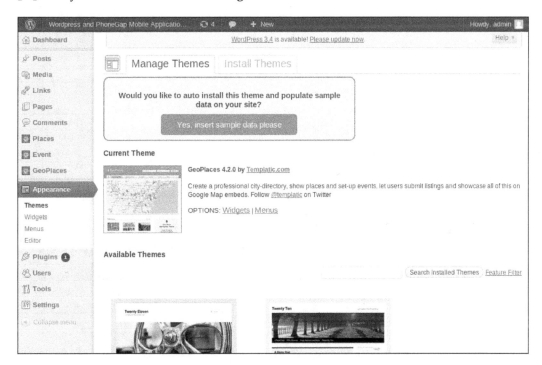

Notice the message box asking if you want to install and populate your site with sample data. Click on the large green button and sample data will automatically be populated. Once done, you should see the following:

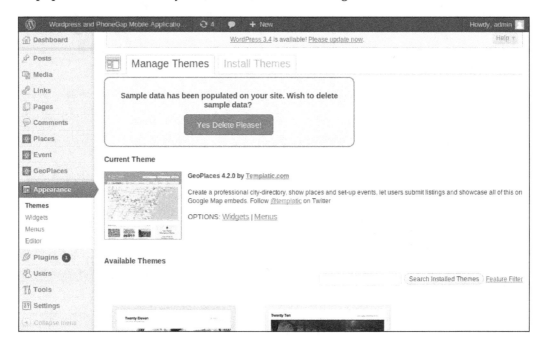

You can choose to delete the sample data should you want to. But for now, let's leave the sample data for browsing purposes.

Playing with sample data

Now that we have populated the site with sample data, its time to explore it.

Checking out cities

With our site populated with sample data, let's take our WordPress site for a spin:

1. First, navigate to your homepage; you should be greeted by a splash page that looks as follows:

2. Now select **New York** and you will be taken to a page with a Google Map that looks like the following screenshot:

3. GeoPlaces leverages on the Google Maps API to provide geographic capabilities to the theme.

4. Feel free to click on the map and other places, such as **Madison Square Park**.

5. If you click on **Madison Square Park** you will see a page that describes **Madison Square Park**. More importantly, on the right hand side of the page, you should see something like the following:

Notice the **Address** row? The address is derived from the Google Maps API. How does it work? Let's try adding a place to find out.

Adding a place from the frontend

Here's how we can add a "place" from the frontend of the site:

1. To add a place, you must first sign in. Sign in from the current page by clicking on the **Sign In** link found at the top right-hand side of the page.

2. Sign in with your credentials. Notice that you remain on the frontend of the site as opposed to the administration side. Now click on the **Add place** link found on the upper right-hand side of the webpage. You should see the following:

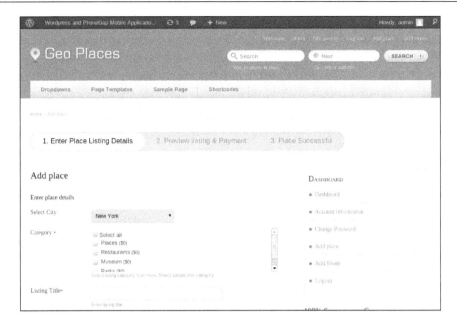

3. You will be greeted by a long webpage that requires you to fill up various fields that are required for listing a page. You should take note of this, as shown in the following screenshot:

4. Try typing `Little Italy` in the **Address** field and click on the **Set address on map** button. You should notice that the map is now marked, and the **Address Latitude** and **Address Longitude** fields are now filled up for you. Your screen for this part of the webpage should now look as follows:

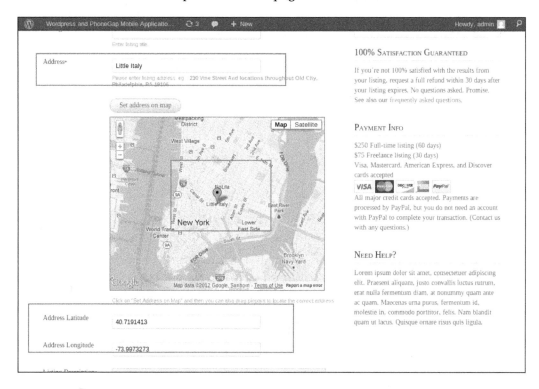

5. The geographically related fields are now filled up.

6. Continue to fill up the other fields, such as the description of this listing, the type of Google map view, special offers, e-mail address, website, and other social media related fields. With these steps, you should have a new place listing in no time.

Adding a place from the admin side

What you have just done is added a place listing from the frontend, as an end user (although you are logged in as admin). So, how do you add a place listing from the admin side of your WordPress site?

1. Firstly, you need to log in to your site if you have not yet done so.

2. Next, navigate to your admin homepage, and go to **Places | Add a Place**. You will see a page that resembles the **Create a New Post** page.

3. Scroll down further and you should notice that the forms filled here are exactly the same as those you see in the frontend of the site. For example, fields for the geographic information are also found on this page:

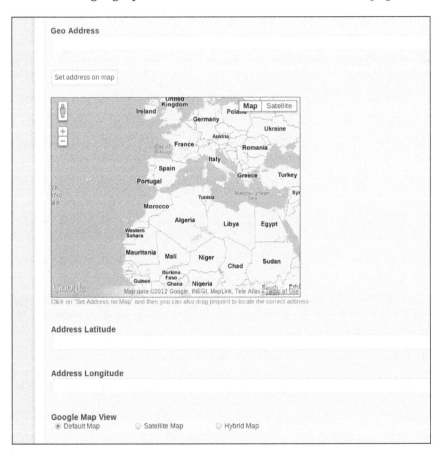

Adding a city from the admin side

To add a city, all you have to do is to log in to the admin side of the site via /wp-admin. Once logged in, go to **GeoPlaces** | **Manage City** and click on **Add City**. From there you'll be able to fill up the details of the city.

Summary

We saw how to manage our WordPress site, covering topics such as populating the site with sample data, adding place listings, and adding a city. You should have a general idea of the geographic capabilities of the theme and how to add a new placelisting. Notice how the theme takes the heavy lifting away by providing built-in geographic functionalities through the Google Maps API.

We also understood how themes and plugins can be used to extend WordPress. In the next chapter we will see how we can extend WordPress and the GeoPlaces theme through the use of JSON-API. Just a heads-up, the JSON-API is used to pull data from our WordPress site into a third-party JavaScript app.

3
Extending WordPress Using JSON-API

In this chapter we will learn how to extend WordPress by using JSON-API. Here are a few things that we will be doing with the JSON-API plugin:

- Extend WordPress by exposing JSON endpoints via WordPress
- Manipulate data through these endpoints by techniques such as reading and creating data

Remember we included some sample data for our WordPress site via the GeoPlaces theme? To set the stage, these sample data will be manipulated using the JSON-API endpoints.

Introducing the JSON-API plugin

The JSON-API plugin can be downloaded from `https://github.com/Achillefs/wp-json-api`. The documentation for the API is found at `http://wordpress.org/extend/plugins/json-api/other_notes/`. Note that we are not using the official plugin, as it does not support creating data from a third-party application. Let us quickly get started by installing the plugin.

Installation

Here's how we can install the plugin:

1. Visit the URL stated in the previous paragraph and download the plugin. Once you have downloaded the plugin, unzip and upload the contents to the `/wp-contents/plugins/` folder.

2. Go to your admin home page and navigate to the plugins page. Activate the JSON-API plugin. Now go to **Settings | JSON API** and you should see the following:

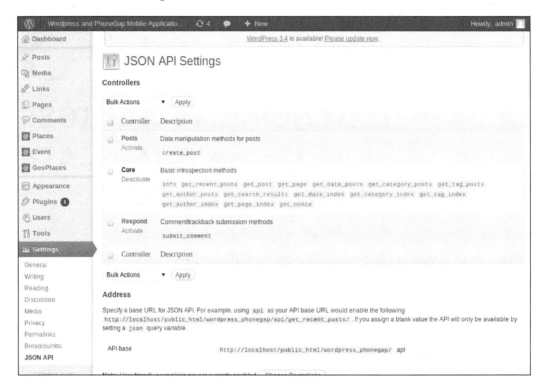

3. Activate the **Posts** controller as we will need it later. Now that we have installed the plugin successfully, let's move on to the next step.

Exploring the JSON-API plugin

For a start, click on the link **get_author_index**; you should see the following:

```
{
    status: "ok",
    count: 1,
  - authors: [
      - {
            id: 1,
            slug: "admin",
            name: "admin",
            first_name: "",
            last_name: "",
            nickname: "admin",
            url: "",
            description: ""
        }
    ]
}
```

Assuming we have the exact same setup, you should also get the above JSON data. Cool, isn't it? This plugin exposes WordPress data in the JSON format. We can also retrieve post information. Try clicking on **get_post** and you will get the following:

```
{
    status: "error",
    error: "Include 'id' or 'slug' var in your request."
}
```

What we need to do here is include an ID in our URL. So assuming we have the exact same setup, let's try to append &id=18 to the end of your URL in the address bar, changing it from /?json=get_post&dev=1 to /?json=get_post&dev=1&id=18. You should now get the following on your screen:

```
{
    status: "error",
    error: "Not found."
}
```

Oops, what happened this time? This error is caused by the fact that the plugin supports default WordPress posts; the GeoPlaces theme will require a different URL argument. Now, if you are seeing the GeoPlaces theme for the first time, feel free to pop back to the previous chapter and go through it.

Now change `/?json=get_post&dev=1&id=18` to `/?json=get_post&dev=1&p=18`. Note that instead of using `id`, we are using `p`. So now refresh your browser and you should see something similar to the following:

```
{
    status: "ok",
  - post: {
        id: 18,
        type: "post",
        slug: "the-cleopatra-girlfriends-weekend-itinerary",
        url: "http://localhost/public_html/wordpress_phonegap/?p=18",
        status: "publish",
        title: "The Cleopatra Girlfriends Weekend Itinerary",
        title_plain: "The Cleopatra Girlfriends Weekend Itinerary",
        content: "<p>Strong, shrewd, beautiful and beguiling, Cleopatra, the last Pharaoh to rule Egypt before the
        completion of the Roman conquest, has been portrayed reverently by historians and Hollywood alike, making her an
        enduring icon and role model to women. As such, the world debut of Cleopatra: The Search for the Last Queen of
        Egypt at The Franklin Institute, which runs from June 5, 2010 through January 2, 2011, will likely resonate with
        thousands of women who admire the ancient queen. It&acute;s also an ideal opportunity to gather friends together
        for a girlfriends</p> ",
        excerpt: "Strong, shrewd, beautiful and beguiling, Cleopatra, the last Pharaoh to rule Egypt before the completion
        of the Roman conquest, has been portrayed reverently by historians and Hollywood alike, making her an enduring icon
        and role model to women. As such, the world debut of Cleopatra: The Search for the Last Queen of Egypt at The
        Franklin Institute, which runs from June 5, 2010 through January 2, 2011, will likely resonate with thousands of
        women who admire the ancient queen. It&acute;s also an ideal opportunity to gather friends together for a
        girlfriends",
        date: "2012-06-21 05:17:38",
        modified: "2012-06-21 05:17:38",
      - categories: [
          - {
                id: 3,
                slug: "blog",
                title: "Blog",
                description: "",
                parent: 0,
                post_count: 11
            }
        ],
      - tags: [
          - {
                id: 9,
                slug: "girlfriends",
                title: "Girlfriends",
                post_count: 1
            }
        ],
      - author: {
            id: 1,
            slug: "admin",
            name: "admin",
            first_name: "",
            last_name: "",
            nickname: "admin",
            url: "",
            description: ""
        },
        comments: [ ],
      - attachments: [
          - {
                id: 19,
                url: "http://localhost/public_html/wordpress_phonegap/?attachment_id=19",
                slug: "img8",
                title: "img8",
                description: "",
                caption: "",
                parent: 18,
                mime_type: "image/jpeg",
              - images: {
                  - full: {
                        url: "http://localhost/public_html/wordpress_phonegap/?attachment_id=19",
                        width: 500,
                        height: 480
                    },
                  - thumbnail: {
                        url: "http://localhost/public_html/wordpress_phonegap/?attachment_id=19",
                        width: 126,
                        height: 185
                    },
                  - medium: {
                        url: "http://localhost/public_html/wordpress_phonegap/?attachment_id=19",
                        width: 300,
                    },
                  - large: {
                        url: "http://localhost/public_html/wordpress_phonegap/?attachment_id=19",
                        width: 500,
                        height: 480
                    },
                  - post-thumbnail: {
                        url: "http://localhost/public_html/wordpress_phonegap/?attachment_id=19",
                        width: 362,
                        height: 250
                    },
                  - loopThumb: {
                        url: "http://localhost/public_html/wordpress_phonegap/?attachment_id=19",
                        width: 151,
                        height: 125
                    }
                }
            }
        ],
        comment_count: 0,
        comment_status: "open"
    },
    previous_url: "http://localhost/public_html/wordpress_phonegap/?p=16",
    next_url: "http://localhost/public_html/wordpress_phonegap/?p=20"
}
```

If you can see the code shown in the earlier screenshot, it's time to move to the next section.

A simple web app to read data

In this section we will write a simple, one-page JavaScript application to manipulate data. This application has two basic operations: reading and creating posts. This application will form the basis for the remainder of this book.

Reading a blog post

We'll start by performing a simple action: reading a blog post.

Creating a Hello World JavaScript app

We will start by first learning how to display the "Hello World" blog post into our simple JavaScript application. We will be using jQuery extensively to do the heavy lifting of Ajax operations.

1. First copy the following code into the app.html file:

    ```
    <!DOCTYPE HTML>
    <html>
    <header>
    <script src="https://ajax.googleapis.com/ajax/libs/jquery/1.7.2/
    jquery.min.js"></script>
    <script>
    jQuery(document).ready(function() {
    jQuery("#title").html("<h1>Hello World</h1>");
    });
    </script>
    </header>
    <body>
    <div id="main">
    <div id="title"></div>
    </div>
    </body>
    </html>
    ```

2. Save this file as app.html. Open this file using your favorite web browser and you'll receive the following message on screen:

Hello World

The "Hello World" is created using JavaScript. Note that we've included jQuery by making use of Google's **Content Delivery Network (CDN)** host of JavaScript libraries.

Once you have seen the previous message, move onto the next step.

Consuming JSON feeds

Now we will move on with consuming the JSON feed. We will be writing a `readSinglePost()` function that performs a `GET` request.

1. Firstly, copy and paste the following code under the opening `<script>` tag:

```
function readSinglePost (url,target_div) {
var URL = url
jQuery.ajax({
url: URL,
dataType: 'json',
success: function(data) {

jQuery(target_div).html(data.post.content);

    }
});
}
```

2. The earlier code takes in a URL that returns a JSON response, and appends the response to the `div #contents` element. For the sake of simplicity, we will append the content of the blog post.

3. In order to use the earlier function, we now call the function with two arguments: the URL and a target `div` element, which in this case is `#contents`. Now add in the highlighted code shown as follows:

```
jQuery(document).ready(function() {
jQuery("#title").html("<h1>Hello World</h1>");
// you might have to change this url
varurl = "http://localhost/public_html/wordpress_
phonegap/?json=get_post&dev=1&p=1";
vartarget_div = "#contents";

readSinglePost(url, target_div);

});
```

Take note that you might have to change the URL if you are using a different directory.

Now save your file and open it in your favorite web browser. You should now see the following:

Hello World

Welcome to WordPress. This is your first post. Edit or delete it, then start blogging!

Notice how the contents of your default "Hello World" blog post are now shown in the earlier screenshot? With the help of the JSON-API plugin and using a few lines of JavaScript, we can show content from your blog on an external application. Now comment out the line jQuery("#title").html("<h1>Hello World</h1>"); and add the following highlighted code in the function readSinglePost(), as shown:

```
function readSinglePost (url,target_div) {
var URL = url//+"&callback=?";
console.log(URL);
jQuery.ajax({
url: URL,
dataType: 'json',
    success: function(data) {
console.log(data);
jQuery(target_div).append("<h1>"+data.post.title+"</h1>");
jQuery(target_div).append(data.post.content);jQuery(target_div).
append("<small>"+data.post.date+"</small>");
console.log(data.post.content);
    }
});
}
```

The highlighted lines of code capture the title, content, and date attribute. Append them to your target_div. Now save your file and refresh your browser, and you should see the following on your screen:

Hello world!

Welcome to WordPress. This is your first post. Edit or delete it, then start blogging!

2012-06-21 05:13:35

If you see the previous screenshot, you are ready to move to the next section.

Paging through blog posts

We have seen how to build a really simple and straightforward example that utilizes a straightforward GET statement to retrieve the data that we have created on our WordPress site.

Paging across the blog post

In this slightly more advanced example, we will be building on the concepts that we have used in the previous example. In a previous example, we used jQuery's `ajax` method to load JSON content into the web application. In this example we will be using it in a similar manner, but we will be adding additional functionality we will enable paging of blog postings in this application.

Copy and paste the following code into the `app_advanced.html` file:

```html
<!DOCTYPE HTML>
<html>
<header>
<script src="https://ajax.googleapis.com/ajax/libs/jquery/1.7.2/
jquery.min.js"></script>
</header>
<body>
<div id="main">
<button type="button" id="previous">Previous</button>
<button type="button" id="next">Next</button>
<div id="title"></div>
<div id="contents"></div>
</div>
</body>
</html>
```

Save this file in your project directory and open it in your favorite web browser. You should see the following:

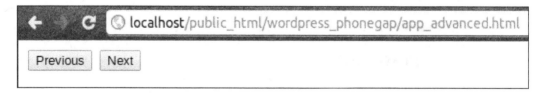

The **Previous** and **Next** buttons will be used to page across blog posts. Now, let us add more functionality to this application; copy and paste the following code before the `</header>`tag:

```
<script>
vartarget_div = "#contents";
varnextID = null;
varprevID = null;
// remember to change the urls in this example
varapi_read_url = "http://localhost/public_html/wordpress_
phonegap/?json=get_post&dev=1&p=";

varinit_url = "http://localhost/public_html/wordpress_
phonegap/?json=get_post&dev=1&p=1";
function getID(url) {
varstr = new String(url)
var x = str.split("=");
var id = x[1];
return id;
}
function readSinglePost (url,target_div) {
var URL = url//+"&callback=?";
console.log(URL);
jQuery.ajax({
url: URL,
dataType: 'json',
    success: function(data) {
jQuery(target_div).html("");
try {
jQuery(target_div).append("<h1>"+data.post.title+"</h1>");
jQuery(target_div).append(data.post.content);
jQuery(target_div).append("<small>"+data.post.date+"</small>");
}
catch (e) {
; // you should include some of your own error-handling code or
messages here.
}
try {
nextID = getID(data.next_url);
}
catch (e) {
; // you should include some of your own error-handling code or
messages here.
}
try {
prevID = getID(data.previous_url);
}
catch (e) {
; // you should include some of your own error-handling code or
```

```
messages here.
      }
        }
});
}

function getNext() {
jQuery("#next").click(function() {
var id = nextID;
varnextURL = api_read_url + id;
readSinglePost(nextURL, target_div);
});
}

function getPrevious() {
jQuery("#previous").click(function() {
var id = prevID;
varprevURL = api_read_url + id;
readSinglePost(prevURL, target_div);
});
}
jQuery(document).ready(function() {
readSinglePost(init_url, target_div);
getNext();
getPrevious();

});
</script>
```

Take note that you may have to change the URL if you have installed WordPress in a different directory than I did.

The previous JavaScript code should look familiar to you. We use the readSinglePost() function, which basically does the same thing as the previous example, except that we have added three try-catch blocks in this function.

The getID() function is used to get the ID of the next or the previous blog post. The getNext() and getPrevious() functions help us obtain the next or previous blog post when the **Next** and **Previous** buttons are clicked.

Now save the file and open it in your favorite web browser; you should see the following:

It is the same as our previous example, except that we have the **Previous** and **Next** buttons on top of the **Hello world!** title. Click on the **Next** button and you should see the following:

Cool, isn't it? You can try to click on these buttons and you will see that the blog post will be loaded according to its post ID. If you click the **Previous** button while on the first post or the **Next** button while on the last post, nothing will happen. This is because the example does not support error handling for this situation.

Now that our application can read blog posts, it's time to see how we can create new blog posts. Let's move on to the next section and see how we can do this.

Creating blog post

Creating blog posts involves two steps: firstly, we need a token from our WordPress website and secondly, we need to post content to the JSON endpoint. The endpoint for getting our token is /?json=get_nonce, and the endpoint for creating a post is /?json=posts/create_post. So let's see how we can do it manually.

Manual creation of posts

In order to create a blog post using JSON-API, WordPress requires you to get a token known as a nonce. Here's how you can create posts manually via JSON-API:

1. Log in to your WordPress admin and go to **Settings | JSON-API**. Look for the **create_post** link as shown in the following screenshot:

2. Click on the **create _post** link and you should see the following message on your screen:

```
  localhost/public_html/wordpress_phonegap/?json=posts/create_post&dev=1
{
    status: "error",
    error: "You must include a 'nonce' value to create posts. Use the `get_nonce` Core API method."
}
```

Now, on the screen append `&controller= post& method= create_post` to the URL on the address bar. Now you should see the following on your screen:

```
{
    status: "ok",
    controller: "posts",
    method: "create_post",
    nonce: "5db25f8e1e"
}
```

Your nonce value can be different from mine. Now go to your WordPress home page and append the following on your URL: `/?json=posts/create_post&dev=1&nonce=5db25f8e1e&title=testing&status=publish`. Remember to use your nonce value. Now reload the page; you should see something like the following if everything is proceeding correctly:

```
{
    status: "ok",
  - post: {
        id: 185,
        type: "post",
        slug: "testing",
        url: "http://localhost/public_html/wordpress_phonegap/?p=185",
        status: "publish",
        title: "testing",
        title_plain: "testing",
        content: "",
        excerpt: "",
        date: false,
        modified: "2012-07-01 11:37:12",
        categories: [ ],
        tags: [ ],
      - author: {
            id: 1,
            slug: "admin",
            name: "admin",
            first_name: "",
            last_name: "",
            nickname: "admin",
            url: "",
            description: ""
        },
        comments: [ ],
        attachments: [ ],
        comment_count: 0,
        comment_status: "open"
    }
}
```

This is your new blog post, created manually. Now that we have understood how the creation of blog posts can be done manually using the JSON-API, this time we will see how we can do it through our application.

Programmatic creation of posts

In order to create post programmatically, we update our application. Now let's see how we can create posts programmatically:

1. Copy and paste the highlighted lines into `app_advanced.html`:

```
..// code truncated
<body>
<div id="main">
<button type="button" id="previous">Previous</button>
<button type="button" id="next">Next</button>
<button type="button" id="create">Create</button>
<div id="form" style="display:none">
Title: <br /><input type="text" name="post_title" id="post_title"
/><br />
Content: <br />
<textarea name="post_contents" id="post_contents"></textarea>
<br />
<input type="submit" value="Submit" id="create_post"/>
```

```
</div>
<div id="title"></div>
<div id="contents"></div>
</div>
</body>
```

Save your application and open it in your favorite web browser. You should see the following on your screen:

2. Now, going back to your code, copy and paste the following JavaScript functions into your <script> tag:

```
// code above truncated

function createButton() {
jQuery("#create").click(function(){
jQuery("#form").toggle();
});
}

function addContent(data) {
// post the content to wordpress
//alert(nounce);
var username = "&author=admin"; // change "admin" to something
else if you are using a different username
varpwd = "&user_password=123456"; // change "123456" to something
else if you are using a different password.
var title = "&title="+jQuery("#post_title").val();
var content = "&content="+jQuery("#post_contents").val();
var post = "http://localhost/public_html/wordpress_
phonegap/?json=posts/create_post&dev=1&status=publish"+pwd+usernam
e+title+content+"&nonce="+data.nonce;
console.log(post);
jQuery.ajax({
url: post,
```

```
    type: "POST",
dataType: 'json',
    success: function(data) {
console.log(data);      }
});
}

function getNonce() {
// retrieve nonce token

varget_nounce_url = "http://localhost/public_html/wordpress_
phonegap/?json=get_nonce&dev=1&controller=posts&method=create_
post";
varnonuce;
jQuery.ajax({
url: get_nounce_url,
    type: "GET",
dataType: 'json',
    success: addContent
});


}

function submitClick() {
jQuery("#create_post").click(function(){
getNonce();
})
}

jQuery(document).ready(function() {readSinglePost(init_url,
target_div);
getNext();
getPrevious();
createButton();
submitClick();
});
```

Take note that you might want to change your username and password to something else if you are not using the same configuration as I am.

The getNonce() function retrieves the token from WordPress. After which the addContent() function is called to create a new blog post. Remember to initialize the createButton() and submitClick() functions as shown in the highlighted lines of code. Now save your code and refresh it on your browser.

3. Click on the **Create** button and you should see a form show up on your screen:

If you see the previous screenshot, it means that everything is going correctly at this point in time.

Now type something into the **Title** and **Content** fields, and click on **Submit**. You should see a **Success** message under the **Submit** button, as shown in the following screenshot:

If you see a **Success** message, it means that a new blog post has been created. In my case I typed **hey you!** and **yeah you!** for the **Title** and **Content** fields respectively. Just to make sure that our blog post has been created, click on the **Next** button a few times. You should come across a post that looks like the following:

And that's it! Our new blog post is now being created programmatically.

Summary

To summarize, we have learnt how to expose WordPress data using the JSON-API plugin. We have also learnt how to manipulate data via the endpoints through a third-party application.

In the next chapter we will be learning about PhoneGap, an open source mobile development tool that allows you to develop native mobile applications using JavaScript.

4
Building Mobile Applications Using PhoneGap

In this chapter, we will focus on building mobile applications using PhoneGap. Here are a few important points before you continue:

- Make sure you have a working Android SDK installation. You may refer to http://developer.android.com/sdk/installing/index.html for an overview of how Android can be installed. At the time of writing this book, RC 20 is the latest Android SDK, so we will be using this version for the rest of the book.

- The IDE I'm using is Eclipse Indigo.

- We will be using PhoneGap 1.9.

While we are using Android as the example in this book, the techniques shown in this book can be applied to other mobile platforms. So let's get started.

Introducing PhoneGap

PhoneGap (http://phonegap.com/) is a mobile open source framework that allows developers to develop native mobile applications using web technologies, such as HTML 5, JavaScript, and CSS in Eclipse IDE. It also supports up to seven major mobile platforms including iOS Android, Web OS, and other major platforms. So that makes it extremely easy for web developers to develop native mobile applications by packaging native APIs via JavaScript.

Getting started

Let's get started with PhoneGap:

1. Download the PhoneGap package at `http://phonegap.com/download/`.

2. Now create a new Android Application Project in your Eclipse IDE by going to **File** | **New** | **Project**. You should see the following screenshot:

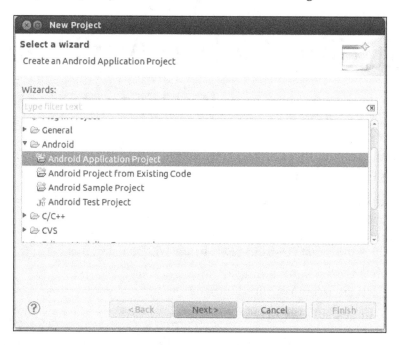

3. Select **Next** and name the new application **HelloWorld**. You should see something similar to the following screenshot:

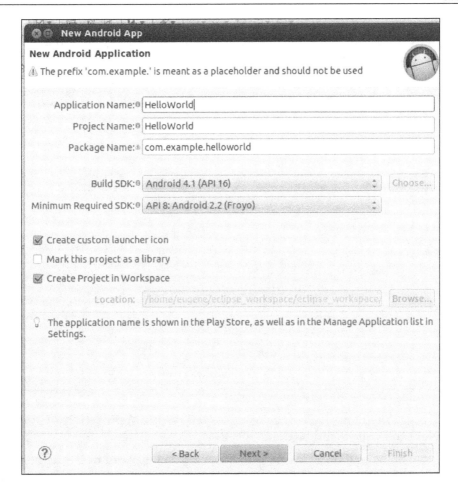

4. Take note that you should also select the appropriate **Build SDK** and **Minimum Required SDK** options as shown in the previous screenshot.

5. Note that the **Build SDK** option is **Android 4.1** and the **Minimum Required SDK** option is **Android 2.2**. Select **Next** and we will be required to create a new activity using the **New Blank Activity** wizard:

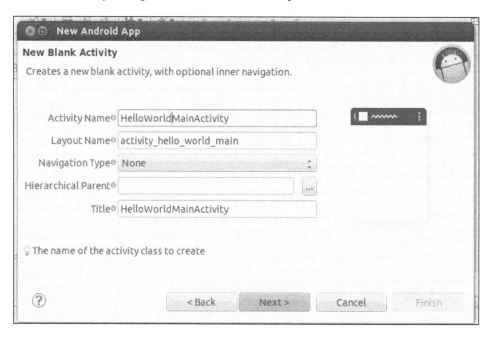

6. The activity name we will be using is **HelloWorldMainActivity**. Click on **Next** and you should be done.

7. Now in the root directory of your project, you will need to create the two new directories /libs and /assets/www. Copy the cordova-1.9.0.js file to the assets/www folder and copy the cordova-1.9.0.jar file to the /libs folder from your PhoneGap package download earlier. Copy the xml folder to /res.

8. Make sure that the cordova-1.9.0.jar file is listed in the path that was built for your project; right-click on the /libs folder and go to **Build Path/| Configure Build Path....| Path....**. Then in the **Libraries** tab click on the **Add JARs** button and add cordova-1.9.0.jar to the project. After adding cordova-1.9.0, press *F5* to refresh your project.

9. Edit your project's main Java file found in the src folder in Eclipse by:
   ° Adding importorg.apache.cordova.*;
   ° Changing the extending class from Activity to DroidGap
   ° Replacing the setContentView() line with super.loadUrl("file:///android_asset/www/index.html");

Your main Java file (`HelloWorldMainActivity.java`) should now look like as follows:

```
package com.example.helloworld;

import android.os.Bundle;
import android.view.Menu;
import org.apache.cordova.*;

public class HelloWorldMainActivity extends DroidGap {

    @Override
    public void onCreate(Bundle savedInstanceState) {
        super.onCreate(savedInstanceState);
        super.loadUrl("file:///android_asset/www/index.html");
    }
}
```

10. Open the `AndroidManifest.xml` file that is found in the root of your project. You may have to open this file using a text editor. Alternatively, you can edit the file in your Eclipse IDE by opening the file in Eclipse IDE followed by clicking on the **AndroidManifest.xml** tab. Now copy the following code between the `<uses-sdk.../>` and `<application.../>` tags into your `AndroidManifest.xml` file:

```
<supports-screens
android:largeScreens="true"
android:normalScreens="true"
android:smallScreens="true"
android:resizeable="true"
android:anyDensity="true" />
<uses-permission android:name="android.permission.VIBRATE" />
<uses-permission android:name="android.permission.ACCESS_COARSE_
LOCATION" />
<uses-permission android:name="android.permission.ACCESS_FINE_
LOCATION" />
<uses-permission android:name="android.permission.ACCESS_LOCATION_
EXTRA_COMMANDS" />
<uses-permission android:name="android.permission.READ_PHONE_
STATE" />
<uses-permission android:name="android.permission.INTERNET" />
<uses-permission android:name="android.permission.RECEIVE_SMS" />
<uses-permission android:name="android.permission.RECORD_AUDIO" />
<uses-permission android:name="android.permission.MODIFY_AUDIO_
SETTINGS" />
```

```
<uses-permission android:name="android.permission.READ_CONTACTS"
/>
<uses-permission android:name="android.permission.WRITE_CONTACTS"
/>
<uses-permission android:name="android.permission.WRITE_EXTERNAL_
STORAGE" />
<uses-permission android:name="android.permission.ACCESS_NETWORK_
STATE" />
<uses-permission android:name="android.permission.GET_ACCOUNTS" />
<uses-permission android:name="android.permission.BROADCAST_
STICKY" />
```

11. To add support for device orientation, copy and paste the following code inside the `<activity>` tag:

```
android:configChanges="orientation|keyboardHidden|screenSize"
```

Creating a Hello World application

Let's now get our hands dirty by coding up a Hello World application:

1. Create an `index.html` file in your `assets/www` folder, and copy and paste the following code into it:

```
<!DOCTYPE HTML>
<html>
<head>
<title>Hello World</title>
<script type="text/javascript" charset="utf-8"src="cordova-
1.9.0.js"></script>
</head>
<body>
<h1>Hello World</h1>
</body>
</html>
```

2. Save the file and right-click on your **HelloWorld** project. Go to **Run As | Android Application**. You will be asked to select an appropriate **Android Virtual Device(AVD)** device if you have not selected one.

3. If you do not have an AVD device, you will be asked to create one. To create an AVD device, you may follow the instructions found at `http://developer.android.com/tools/devices/index.html`. Do not worry if your Android emulator is taking a long time (such as several minutes) to start; sometimes it just happens. If everything is running smoothly, you will see the following screenshot:

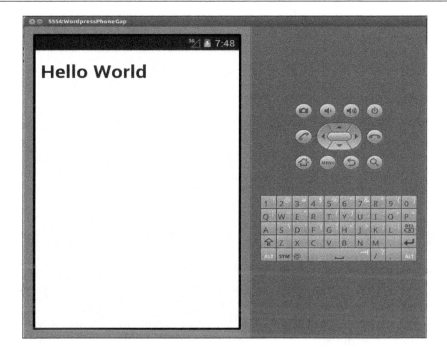

4. Congratulations! Your Hello World example is up and running.

Using jQuery in PhoneGap

Using jQuery in PhoneGap applications is extremely easy; copy and paste the highlighted line as shown in the following code:

```
<!DOCTYPE HTML>
<html>
<head>
<title>Hello World</title>
<script type="text/javascript" charset="utf-8"src="cordova-
1.9.0.js"></script>
<script src="https://ajax.googleapis.com/ajax/libs/jquery/1.7.2/
jquery.min.js"></script>
<script src="https://ajax.googleapis.com/ajax/libs/jquery/1.7.2/
jquery.min.js"></script>
</head>
<body>
<h1>Hello World</h1>
</body>
</html>
```

That's it! You have just installed jQuery. Seems easy enough, doesn't it? While it may seem so, there are some caveats:

1. We are assuming that the application has mobile access, and hence access to the hosted jQuery file. If there's no mobile access, then jQuery will not be downloaded.

2. This method ignores whitelisting, especially in the case of iOS (if you intend to apply the techniques in this book to iOS-based mobile applications), which assures no remote access unless explicitly overridden by the user. For more information on whitelisting, you might want to check out `http://docs. phonegap.com/en/1.9.0/guide_whitelist_index.md.html`.

Performing a RESTful GET request in the PhoneGap application

Since we will be making use of the JSON-API plugin to extend our WordPress blog, let us build a teaser example here; we will be performing a RESTful GET request in our PhoneGap application to get a Hello World post from our WordPress blog, which we have created earlier.

1. Going back to our example in *Chapter 3, Extending WordPress Using JSON-API*, open the `app.html` file and copy the following code snippet:

```
<div id="main">
<div id="title"></div>
<div id="contents"></div>
</div>
```

2. Now paste it in the main `index.html` file of your PhoneGap application, as follows:

```
<!DOCTYPE HTML>
<html>
<head>
<title>Hello World</title>
<script type="text/javascript" charset="utf-8"src="cordova-
1.9.0.js"></script>
<script src="https://ajax.googleapis.com/ajax/libs/jquery/1.7.2/
jquery.min.js"></script>
</head>
<body>
<h1>Hello World</h1>
<div id="main">
<div id="title"></div>
<div id="contents"></div>
```

```
</div>
</body>
</html>
```

3. Next, go back to your `app.html` file and copy the following JavaScript code:

```
<script>
function getNextID(url) {
varstr = new String(url)
alert(str.charAt( str.length-1 ));
return;
}
function readSinglePost (url,target_div) {
var URL = url//+"&callback=?";
console.log(URL);
jQuery.ajax({
url: URL,
dataType: 'json',
    success: function(data) {
console.log(data);
jQuery(target_div).append("<h1>"+data.post.title+"</h1>");
jQuery(target_div).append(data.post.content);
jQuery(target_div).append("<small>"+data.post.date+"</small>");
console.log(data.post.content);
    }
});
}


jQuery(document).ready(function() {
// jQuery("#title").html("<h1>Hello World</h1>");
// you might have to change this url
varurl = "http://localhost/public_html/wordpress_
phonegap/?json=get_post&dev=1&p=1";
vartarget_div = "#contents";

readSinglePost(url, target_div);

getNextID(url);

});
</script>
```

4. Paste it under `<scriptsrc="https://ajax.googleapis.com/ajax/libs/jquery/1.7.2/jquery.min.js"></script>`in the main `index.html` file of your PhoneGap application, and change the line `varurl="http://localhost/public_html/wordpress_phonegap/?json=get_post&dev=1&p=1";` to `varurl="http://10.0.2.2/public_html/wordpress_phonegap/?json=get_post&dev=1&p=1";`.

5. Note that `localhost` has been changed to `10.0.2.2`; this is because `10.0.2.2` is the IP address where you can access your `localhost` from the Android emulator.

   An important point to note here is that the previously mentioned changes will only work on Android emulators. If you are running a real Android application, you will need to change `localhost` to the IP address or domain name of your application.

   Another point to take note of is that the URL `http://10.0.2.2/public_html/wordpress_phonegap/?json=get_post&dev=1&p=1` should be changed to reflect your settings.

6. Now save your main `index.html` file and run your project as an Android application. If everything goes correctly, you will get something like the following screenshot on your Android emulator:

Note that the content from your "Hello World" post is now being captured and shown on our PhoneGap application.

Congratulations! Your PhoneGap application can now perform a RESTful GET request. This is an important building block for the remainder of the book. Now let us quickly check out PhoneGap's Geolocation API.

Capturing geolocation using PhoneGap API

In this section, we will quickly run through how we can capture geolocation information using the PhoneGap's API. We will be modifying some code from PhoneGap's official documentation at http://docs.phonegap.com/en/1.9.0/cordova_geolocation_geolocation.md.html#geolocation.getCurrentPosition.

Let's see how we can start:

1. Create a new HTML file and name it phonegap.html. Save it under your assets/www folder. Copy and paste the following code into the phonegap.html file:

```
<!DOCTYPE html>
<html>
<head>
<title>Device Properties Example</title>
<script type="text/javascript" charset="utf-8"src="cordova-
1.9.0.js"></script>
<script type="text/javascript" charset="utf-8">
// Wait for Cordova to load
//document.addEventListener("deviceready", onDeviceReady, false );
// Cordova is ready
//

function onDeviceReady() {
navigator.geolocation.getCurrentPosition(onSuccess, onError, {
maximumAge: 3000, timeout: 5000, enableHighAccuracy: true });
}


// onSuccessGeolocation
//function onSuccess(position) {
var element = document.getElementById('geolocation');
element.innerHTML = 'Latitude: ' + position.coords.latitude + '<br
/>' +
```

```
'Longitude: ' + position.coords.longitude + '<br />' +
'Altitude: ' + position.coords.altitude + '<br />' +
'Accuracy: ' + position.coords.accuracy + '<br />' +
'Altitude Accuracy: ' + position.coords.altitudeAccuracy + '<br
/>' +
'Heading: ' + position.coords.heading + '<br />' +
'Speed: ' + position.coords.speed + '<br />' +
'Timestamp: ' + position.timestamp + '<br />';
}
// onError Callback receives a PositionError object
//function onError(error) {
alert('code: ' + error.code + '\n' +
'message: ' + error.message + '\n');
}
</script>
</head>
<body>
<p id="geolocation">Finding geolocation...</p>
</body>
</html>
```

2. Save the file. Now go to your `HelloWorldMainActivity.java` file and change `super.loadUrl("file:///android_asset/www/index.html");` to `super.loadUrl("file:///android_asset/www/phonegap.html");`.

3. Now launch your project as an Android application. You should see some geolocation information on your Android emulator:

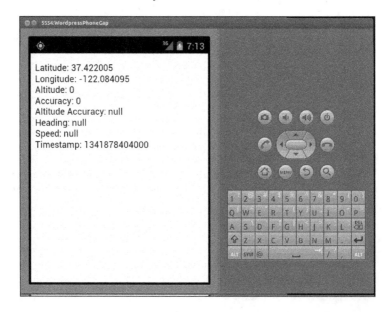

4. If you are seeing the messages that are shown in the earlier screenshot, then congratulations; you have just captured geolocation information using PhoneGap's API.

If you've visited the link (`http://docs.phonegap.com/en/1.9.0/cordova_geolocation_geolocation.md.html#geolocation.getCurrentPosition`) that was referred to earlier, you will see that all quotes differ slightly from the visual code example. The difference is found at the highlighted line where the additional options `{maximumAge:3000,timeout:5000,enableHighAccuracy:true}` are used. The `enableHighAccuracy:true` option is used as there is a quirk with Android where geolocation information will not be returned unless set to `enableHighAccuracy:true`.

If you are having problems with getting the geolocation information, you might have to set this information manually:

1. *Assuming* you are using the Eclipse IDE, navigate to **Window | Open Perspective | DDMS** and you should be presented with the following screenshot:

2. Once your Android emulator is up and running, you should click on the **Send** button; this will simulate the geographic information for your PhoneGap application.

Summary

To summarize, we have learned how to set up PhoneGap in the Eclipse IDE environment. We've also developed a Hello World PhoneGap application. Most importantly, we learned how to perform a RESTful GET request from our PhoneGap application; this functionality forms the bread and butter of our final project in the next chapter. Lastly, we also briefly went through PhoneGap's Geolocation API, which we will be using in the next chapter as well.

In the next chapter, we will learn how to apply the techniques learned in this chapter in tandem with jQuery Mobile. We will also learn how to quickly transit from jQuery to jQuery Mobile.

5

Extending WordPress to the Mobile World

In the last chapter we learned about how we can build mobile applications using PhoneGap. Now, we will continue from *Chapter 4*, *Building Mobile Applications Using PhoneGap* and extend it to work with our GeoPlaces WordPress website. By now, you should be able to see that JSON-APIs work as a form of "glue" that allows desktop websites (in our case, a WordPress website) to have bidirectional interaction with mobile apps.

We will first quickly go through jQuery Mobile, after which we will extend our PhoneGap app, created in *Chapter 3*, *Extending WordPress Using JSON-API* and *Chapter 4*, *Building Mobile Applications Using PhoneGap*.

Introducing jQuery Mobile

jQuery Mobile (http://jquerymobile.com/) is a unified HTML5-based user interface for most popular mobile device platforms. It is based on jQuery (http://jquery.com/) and jQuery UI (http://jqueryui.com/). Our focus in this section is on jQuery Mobile, so let's get our hands dirty. We'll start by implementing jQuery Mobile using the example we created in *Chapter 3*, *Extending WordPress Using JSON-API*.

Installing jQuery Mobile and theming

Installing jQuery Mobile is straightforward and easy:

1. Open up `app_advanced.html` and copy and paste the following code directly within the `<head>` tags:

    ```
    <meta name="viewport" content="width=device-width, initial-
    scale=1">
    <link rel="stylesheet" href="http://code.jquery.com/mobile/1.1.1/
    jquery.mobile-1.1.1.min.css" />
    <script src="http://code.jquery.com/jquery-1.7.1.min.js">
    </script>
    <script src="http://code.jquery.com/mobile/1.1.1/jquery.mobile-
    1.1.1.min.js">
    </script>
    <script src="https://ajax.googleapis.com/ajax/libs/jquery/1.7.2/
    jquery.min.js">
    </script>
    ```

2. Now save your code and open up `app_advanced.html` in your favourite browser. You should be seeing the following screen:

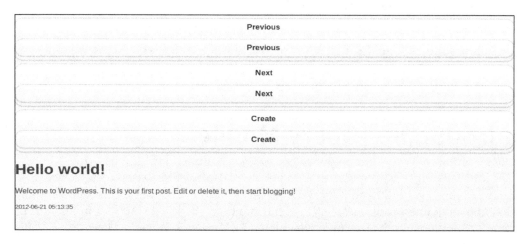

Well, it looks like the webpage has gotten some form of theming, but it looks a little weird. This is because we have not implemented various HTML elements required for jQuery Mobile.

Again, as mentioned in the previous chapter, the code sample assumes that your app has Internet access and hence access to jQuery and jQuery Mobile's CDN. This might reduce the app's startup time. To avoid the problem related to having no network or flaky connectivity, one basic thing you can do is to package your app together with a local copy of jQuery and jQuery Mobile.

Let us move on to the next section and see how we can fix this.

jQuery Mobile page template

Let's go back to `app_advanced.html` and do some editing. Let us focus on the HTML elements found within `<body>` tags; change them to look like the following code snippet:

```
<div id="main" data-role="page">
  <div data-role="header">
    <div data-role="controlgroup"  data-type="horizontal">
      <a href="#" id="previous" data-role="button">Previous</a>
      <a href="#" id="next" data-role="button">Next</a>
      <!-- <button type="button" id="create" data-
role="button">Create</button> -->
      <a href="#create_form" data-role="button" data-
transition="slide">Create</a>
    </div>
  </div>



    <div id="contents" data-role="content"></div>


</div>
<div data-role="page" id="create_form" data-theme="c">
  <div data-role="header" addBackBtn="true">
    <a href="#" data-rel="back">Back</a>
    <h1>Create a new Post</h1>
  </div>
  <div id="form" style="padding:15px;">
    Title: <br /><input type="text" name="post_title" id="post_
title" /><br />
    Content: <br />
```

```
        <textarea name="post_contents" id="post_contents"></textarea>
        <br />
        <input type="submit" value="Submit" id="create_post"/>
        <div id="message"></div>
      </div>

    </div>
```

Now save your code and open it in your favourite web browser. You should see the following screen:

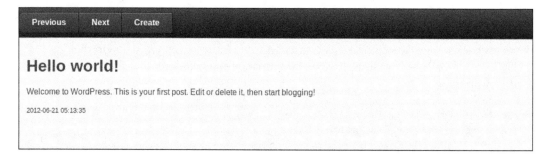

The app now looks great! Feel free to click on the **Next** button and see how the app works.

How does this all work? For a start, check out the highlighted lines of code. In the world of HTML5, the additional lines of HTML code we wrote, such as `data-role="page"` or `data-theme="c"`, are known as custom data attributes. jQuery Mobile makes use of these specifications to denote the things we need in our mobile web app. For example, `data-role="page"` denotes that this particular element (in our case, a `div` element) is a page component. Similarly, `data-theme="c"` in our case refers to a particular CSS style. For more information about data theme, feel free to check out `http://jquerymobile.com/test/docs/content/content-themes.html`.

Animation effects

Now let us try a little bit with animation effects. We can create animation effects by simply leveraging what we know with jQuery. What about jQuery Mobile? There are several animation effects that are distinct to jQuery Mobile, and in this section we will try out animation effects in terms of page transitions.

We will create a page transition effect using the following steps:

1. Click on the **Create** button, and we will get a page transition effect to a new page, where we see our post creation form.

2. On this **Create a new Post** form, as usual, type in some appropriate text in the **Title** and **Content** fields.

3. Finally, click on the **Submit** button.

Let's see how we can achieve the page transition effect:

1. We need to make changes to our code. For the sake of simplicity, delete all HTML code found within your <body> tags in app_advanced.html, and then copy the following code into your <body> tags:

```html
<div id="main" data-role="page">
  <div data-role="header">
    <div data-role="controlgroup"  data-type="horizontal">
      <a href="#" id="previous" data-role="button">Previous</a>
      <a href="#" id="next" data-role="button">Next</a>
      <!-- <button type="button" id="create" data-
role="button">Create</button> -->
      <a href="#create_form" data-role="button" data-
transition="slide">Create</a>
    </div>
  </div>


    <div id="contents" data-role="content"></div>


  </div>
  <div data-role="page" id="create_form" data-theme="c">
    <div data-role="header" addBackBtn="true">
      <a href="#" data-rel="back">Back</a>
      <h1>Create a new Post</h1>
    </div>
    <div id="form" style="padding:15px;">
      Title: <br /><input type="text" name="post_title" id="post_
title" /><br />
      Content: <br />
      <textarea name="post_contents" id="post_contents"></
textarea>
      <br />
      <input type="submit" value="Submit" id="create_post"/>
      <div id="message"></div>
```

```
        </div>

        </div>
```

2. Take note that we have used the `transition="slide"` attribute, so we have a "slide" effect. For more details or options, visit `http://jquerymobile.com/test/docs/pages/page-transitions.html`.

3. Now, save your code and open it in your favorite web browser. Click on the **Create** button, and you will first see a slide transition, followed by the post creation form, as follows:

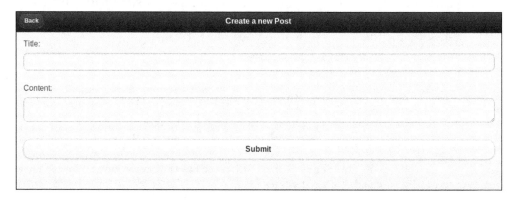

4. Now type in some text, and you will see that jQuery Mobile takes care of the CSS effects in this form as well:

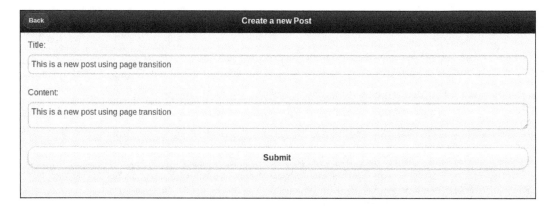

5. Now click on the **Submit** button, and you will see a **Success** message below the **Submit** button, as shown in the following screenshot:

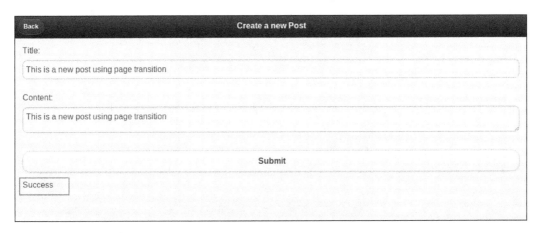

6. If you see the **Success** message, as shown in the earlier screenshot, congratulations! We can now move on to extending our PhoneGap app, which we built in *Chapter 4, Building Mobile Applications Using PhoneGap*.

Extending our PhoneGap app

In this section, we will truly see the power of jQuery Mobile and PhoneGap. Now, in order to use the code that we have made in the previous section, all we have to do is port it over to our PhoneGap application:

1. Go to your Eclipse editor and open up the main Java file. If you have been following the instructions up to this point, the name of the file should be `HelloWorldMainActivity.java`. Change the `super.loadUrl("file://android_asset/www/phonegap.html")` statement in the code file to `super.loadUrl("file://android_asset/www/chapter5.html")`.

2. Next, create a new file called `chapter5.html` in your `assets/www` folder. Copy and paste the code from `app_advanced.html` into `chapter5.html`. Save the file.

3. Now, there is one important thing to take note of: since we are going to run our code in an Android emulator, we need to change the the URL at which we read the content or post content to our WordPress site. Therefore, change all instances of `http://localhost` to `http://10.0.2.2`, in the code found in `chapter5.html`.

4. Once you are done, save `chapter5.html`. Start your project as an Android project, and you should see the following:

5. Click on **Next**, and you should see the following:

6. Now, let us test out the page transition effect by clicking on the **Create** button. You should see a page transition effect and see the post creation form as shown in the following screenshot:

Posting data to a JSON endpoint in PhoneGap

In the previous section we have tested out the functionalities in our PhoneGap app, which we have coded in `app_advanced.html`. What about posting data to a JSON endpoint? Does it work? Let's find out!

1. Continuing in our Android emulator, let us type some text in the **Title** and **Content** fields:

2. Now click on **Submit**, and you should see a **Success** message as per what we have seen using `app_advanced.html`:

3. If you see the **Success** message, it's time to move on. If not, you might want to check your code and make sure that `http://localhost` has been changed to `http://10.02.2`.

Putting everything together with the GeoPlaces theme

Now that we have seen how we can quickly convert a simple JavaScript/HTML app into a PhoneGap app, it's time to see how we can tie all these skills together and put them to use. We will now attempt to perform similar operations based on features unique to the GeoPlaces theme: read places data and post places data into our GeoPlaces WordPress app.

Before we start, we need to hack into the JSON-API plugin, as it doesn't support the input of `custom_fields` while creating posts.

Hacking the JSON-API plugin

Follow these steps to hack into the JSON-API plugin:

1. Navigate to your `wp-content/plugins` folder and open up the `JSON-API` plugin folder. Then, go into the `Controllers` folder and open the `posts.php` file.

2. Check out the public function `create_post()`, and search for the following code lines:

   ```
   if (empty($id)) {
   $json_api->error("Could not create post.");
   }
   ```

3. Under this `if` block, we will add the following `else` block:

   ```
   else {
   $geo_address_value = $_REQUEST['geo_address_value'];
   $geo_latitude_value = $_REQUEST['geo_latitude_value'];
   $geo_longitude_value = $_REQUEST['geo_longitude_value'];
   add_post_meta($id,"geo_address", $geo_address_value);
   add_post_meta($id,"geo_latitude", $geo_latitude_value);
   add_post_meta($id,"geo_longitude", $geo_longitude_value);
   }
   ```

Now save this file and move on to the next step.

 Since we are making changes to the JSON-API plugin, keep in mind that you'll need to make the same changes as seen in this section after upgrading the plugin.

Powering your PhoneGap app

For a start, create a new file in your PhoneGap project under the `assets/www` folder. Name this file `chapter5_advanced.html`. In general, the code structure for this file is very similar to what we have done so far in the previous section, but with a few subtle changes.

Firstly, copy and paste the code in `chapter5.html` into `chapter5_advanced.html`. Save this file. Next, go to your main Java file and change the `super.loadUrl(file://android_asset/www/chapter5.html)` statement from the code file to `super.loadUrl(file://android_asset/www/chapter5_advanced.html)`.

Now let us make a few changes to the code in `chapter5_advanced.html`:

1. Go to the `<body>` section and search for the line `<textarea name="post_ contents" id="post_contents"></textarea><br />`. Beneath this line, add the following code snippet:

```
Address: <br /><input type="text" name="geo_address_value"
id="geo_address_value" /><br />
Latitude: <br /><input type="text" name="geo_latitude_value"
id="geo_latitude_value" /><br />
Longitude: <br /><input type="text" name="geo_longitude_value"
id="geo_longitude_value" /><br />
```

This code is to add in the required input fields for geographic information.

2. Next, go to your JavaScript code, and look for the function `addContent(data)`. Search for the line `var content = "&content="+jQuery("#post_contents").val();`. Under this line of code, copy and paste the following JavaScript code:

```
Vargeo_address_value = "&geo_address_value="+jQuery("#geo_address_
value").val();
vargeo_latitude_value = "&geo_latitude_value="+jQuery("#geo_
latitude_value").val();
vargeo_longtitude_value = "&geo_longtitude_value="+jQuery("#geo_
longitude_value").val();
varpost = "http://10.0.2.2/public_html/wordpress_
phonegap/?json=posts/create_post&dev=1&status=publish&type=pla
ce"+pwd+username+title+content+geo_address_value+geo_latitude_
value+geo_longtitude_value+"&nonce="+data.nonce;
```

Here we are adding in JavaScript variables to capture the geographic information and posting it to our JSON endpoint.

3. The next function we are going to edit is the `readSinglePost()` function. We will be adding in a few lines of code to enable reading of geographic information from posts that are of place type. So add in the following lines of code under `jQuery(target_div).append("<p>"+data.post.content+"</p>");`, which is found in the try-catch code block:

```
jQuery(target_div).append("<p>"+data.post.custom_fields.geo_
address+"</p>");
jQuery(target_div).append("<p>"+data.post.custom_fields.geo_
latitude+"</p>");
jQuery(target_div).append("<p>"+data.post.custom_fields.geo_
longitude+"</p>");
```

4. Finally, let us make some changes to the `api_read_url` and `init_url` variables found at the beginning of this JavaScript code. These variables should look like the following:

```
varapi_read_url = "http://10.0.2.2/public_html/wordpress_
phonegap/?json=get_post&custom_fields=geo_address,geo_
latitude,geo_longitude&dev=1&type=place&place=";
varinit_url = "http://10.0.2.2/public_html/wordpress_
phonegap/?json=get_post&&custom_fields=geo_address,geo_
latitude,geo_longitude&dev=1&p=114&type=place";
```

5. Save the file. We are now all set to test out these functions. Start the PhoneGap project as an Android project, and you should see the following on your Android emulator:

6. Scroll down this screen, and you should see the following geographic information:

7. If you are seeing this, great! Our function that reads posts of place type now works. Try clicking on the **Next** button, and you should see some other information that we have created in the previous chapters, such as that shown in the following screenshot:

8. The earlier post was created via WordPress's admin (if you still remember it).

9. Now, let us click on the **Create** button and see what we've got:

10. If you are seeing the preceding screenshot in your **Create a new Post** form, you are on the right track. Now, let us type some basic information and click on the **Submit** button:

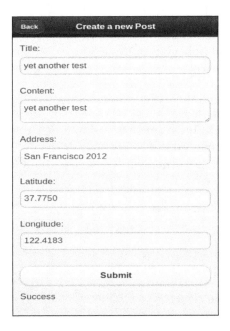

11. As expected, we see the **Success** message. Close the Android emulator and start it up again. Once the app has loaded, click on the **Next** button one or two times, and you should see the post that we created earlier, complete with geographic information:

12. If you are seeing the preceding screen, congratulations! The app now works! You can easily manipulate the sample code here to get geographic input from Google Maps or simply use the latitude and longitude information and feed it into a mapping server to create a visually pleasing mobile web app.

Summary

You have successfully applied what you have learned from the first four chapters, and some new techniques from this chapter, to build a mobile app from the ground up while leveraging with PhoneGap, jQuery, jQuery Mobile, and WordPress. Notice how these open source projects provided the bulk of the heavy lifting in our coding process. Cool, isn't it?

Now certain readers out there might ask, "What about those people who do not use the GeoPlaces theme? Can we apply the techniques in this book to a generic or even to open source or free themes?" My answer to you is a resounding "Yes!" In the next chapter, we'll apply whatever we have learned in the first five chapters to the standard open source theme that all WordPress installations come with, the Twenty Ten theme.

6
Using Open Source Themes

In this chapter, we will focus on applying the techniques we have learnt in the first five chapters on open source themes. The theme we have chosen for this chapter is the default Twenty Ten theme that comes with all WordPress installations.

General idea

Let's quickly go through what we have done in order to create a PhoneGap application out of WordPress. In general, our strategy can be summarized as follows:

1. Install WordPress and the JSON-API plugin.

2. Build a web application that can read and write blog posts to our WordPress installation. We can choose to apply jQuery, jQuery Mobile, or any other JavaScript libraries that makes development easier.

3. Convert the web application to a PhoneGap app. While converting, take note that `http://localhost` has to be changed to `http://10.0.2.2`, since we will be performing read and post operations from the Android emulator.

In the next section, that is exactly what we will be doing. We will be reusing the code we have written in *Chapter 5*, *Extending WordPress to the Mobile World*, to illustrate how easily the strategy can be applied to other themes.

Creating a PhoneGap Mobile app using the Twenty Ten theme

In this section, we'll see how we can build a mobile app using the techniques we have learned in the previous chapters and apply them on an open source theme, the Twenty Ten theme.

Switching to the Twenty Ten theme

We need to switch to the Twenty Ten theme, using the following steps:

1. Log in to your WordPress admin, and go to **Appearance | Themes | Manage Themes**.

2. Select and activate the **Twenty Ten** theme.

3. Once you have activated the theme, your WordPress website should look as follows:

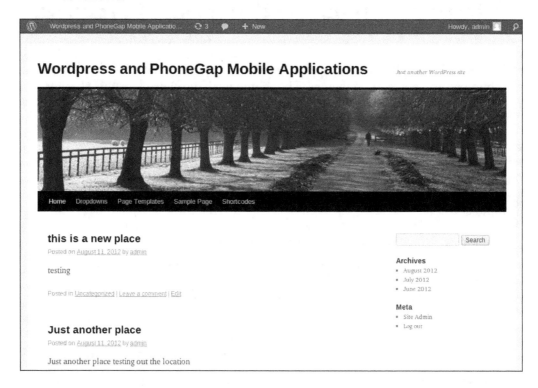

Custom fields

If you are using a fresh installation of WordPress, make sure to create your required custom fields that you need before attempting to create a post via the JSON-API. If you have been following the book, your JSON-API plugin now supports custom fields, but only a few specific ones.

To check if you have certain custom fields follow these steps:

1. Log in to your WordPress admin page, go to **Posts**, and click on any posts.

2. If your custom fields are available and some of them are already filled up, you should see something like the following screenshot:

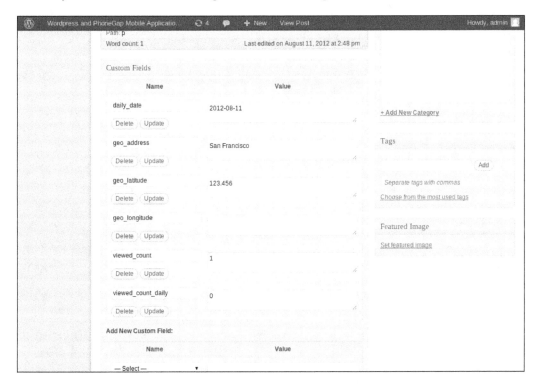

3. If your custom fields are not filled up, for instance the **Hello World** post, you will get a drop-down box that displays a list of custom fields available for you. In case you do not see the custom fields list at all, be sure to scroll to the top of this page and check on a select box and click on the **Custom Fields** checkbox.

4. Should you want to modify any of the custom fields via the JSON-API, make sure to edit JSON-API's code, as shown in *Chapter 5, Extending WordPress to the Mobile World*.

Reading from and writing to WordPress

We'll now start by creating a web app that reads and writes to WordPress. Since the concept is strikingly similar to what we have done for the GeoPlaces theme, we can make use of the code we have written in *Chapter 5*. Let's copy and paste the code we have written in `chapter5_advanced.html`, into a new file called `chapter6_webapp.html`.

Preamble

Before we can start posting data with `custom_fields` to our WordPress site, we need to make some changes to the code we have written in *Chapter 5, Extending WordPress to the Mobile World*. For a start, locate the following lines:

```
var api_read_url = "http://localhost/public_html/wordpress_
phonegap/?json=get_post&custom_fields=geo_address,geo_latitude,geo_lon
gitude&dev=1&type=place&place=";
var init_url = "http://localhost/public_html/wordpress_
phonegap/?json=get_post&&custom_fields=geo_address,geo_
latitude,geo_longitude&dev=1&p=114&type=place";
```

Edit them to mimic the following code snippet:

```
var api_read_url = "http://localhost/public_html/wordpress_
phonegap/?json=get_post&custom_fields=geo_address,geo_
latitude,geo_longitude&dev=1&p=";
var init_url = "http://localhost/public_html/wordpress_
phonegap/?json=get_post&&custom_fields=geo_address,geo_
latitude,geo_longitude&dev=1&p=1";
```

We also need to change the following lines in our code file:

```
var post = "http://localhost/public_html/wordpress_
phonegap/?json=posts/create_post&dev=1&status=publish&type=place"+p
wd+username+title+content+geo_address_value+geo_latitude_value+geo_
longtitude_value+"&nonce="+data.nonce;
```

Mimic the following code snippet:

```
var post = "http://localhost/public_html/wordpress_
phonegap/?json=posts/create_post&dev=1&status=publish"+pwd+use
rname+title+content+geo_address_value+geo_latitude_value+geo_
longtitude_value+"&nonce="+data.nonce;
```

What we have done is to remove the `type=place` attribute and also to change the initial post ID to 1. We are doing this because we are going to perform bare-bones read and post operations to our WordPress website.

Once you are done with this, save the file and move on to the next section.

Creating a post with custom fields

Let us create some posts before we read them. As usual, we are going to create a post with custom fields. Let's look at how we can do that:

1. Start by opening up `chapter6.html` in your favorite browser.
2. Click on the **Create** button, and then start filling up the form.
3. Finally, click on **Submit**. You should see a **Success** message, as shown in the following screenshot:

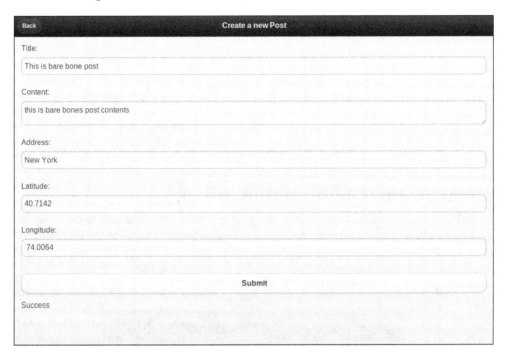

Now, let us check out the code that is responsible for the success in creating the post:

```
function addContent(data) {

    var username = "&author=admin";
    var pwd = "&user_password=123456";
    var title = "&title="+jQuery("#post_title").val();
    var content = "&content="+jQuery("#post_contents").val();
    var geo_address_value = "&geo_address_value="+jQuery("#geo_
address_value").val();
    var geo_latitude_value = "&geo_latitude_value="+jQuery("#geo_
latitude_value").val();
    var geo_longtitude_value = "&geo_longtitude_value="+jQuery("#geo_
longitude_value").val();
    var post = "http://localhost/public_html/wordpress_
phonegap/?json=posts/create_post&dev=1&status=publish&type=place"+p
wd+username+title+content+geo_address_value+geo_latitude_value+geo_
longtitude_value+"&nonce="+data.nonce;
```

```
jQuery.ajax({
    url: post,
    type: "POST",
    dataType: 'json',
    success: function(data) {

    jQuery("#message").html("<p>Success</p>");
    }
  });
}
```

The addContent() function is exactly the same that we have been using for the previous chapter. The only things we have changed are the URLs that we edited in the earlier section. The addContent() function is called from the getNonce() function, which is in turn called by the submitClick() function. These are the exact same strategies and logic that we used in *Chapter 5, Extending WordPress to the Mobile World*.

Reading a post with custom fields

Now that we have created a post with geographic data, let us see if we can read it. Click on the **Back** button, which should take you to the first post of your blog, the "Hello World" blog post. Depending on the ID of your post, keep clicking next until you see the following (assuming you have typed the same information as I did) on your screen:

If you got the preceding screen, congratulations! You now have a working web app that allows you to read and post blog posts with custom_fields data to your WordPress blog.

Next, let us shift the code to our PhoneGap project, such that we can build a mobile application.

Building an Android PhoneGap app

Shifting your web app to PhoneGap is very simple. Let's get started.

Shifting your web app code to PhoneGap

We'll start by creating `chapter6_phonegap.html` in your `assets/www` folder, in your PhoneGap project. Change the line `super.loadUrl("file:///android_ asset/www/chapter5_advanced.html");` to `super.loadUrl("file:/// android_asset/www/chapter6_phonegap.html");` in your main Java file (`HelloWorldMainActivity.java`). Next, copy and paste the code in `chapter6_webapp.html` to `chapter6_phonegap.html`.

Now here's an important step that we have done before: change all instances of `http://localhost` to `http://10.0.2.2` since we are going to read and post data from the Android emulator. Again, take note that `http://10.0.2.2` only applies to the Android emulator and not a physical device or another platform. If you are using Eclipse, you can perform a "find and replace all" action to do this.

Creating a post with custom fields

Let us create some posts before we read them. As usual, we are going to create a post with custom fields. So in order to do that, start your Android emulator, click on the **Create** button, and then start filling up the form. Finally, click on **Submit**. You should see a **Success** message as in the following screenshot:

The code responsible for performing this action is exactly what we have been using.

Reading a post with custom fields

Now that we have created a post on the Android emulator, let us try and read it. Click on the **Back** button, and you should be greeted with the "Hello World" post. As with the preceding section, we will need to click on **Next** a few times and see if our post can be read successfully. If everything goes smoothly, you should see the following (assuming you posted the same information that I did) on your screen:

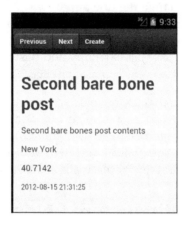

If you see something like the preceding screenshot, everything is working perfectly.

Summary

Notice how the strategy used in applying the techniques learned from the first five chapters is similar to the one used to apply on an open source theme. We are leveraging on `custom_fields` to provide us with customized data, while performing the same action of creating and reading posts via the JSON-API.

The main thing to take note, when replicating your code for the web to PhoneGap is the change in URL from `http://localhost` to `http://10.0.2.2`, since we are attempting to read and post data from the Android emulator.

With that, we have come to the end of this book. I hope you have learned a lot and seen the power of using WordPress and the JSON-API plugin together with PhoneGap. As a reminder, the support for this book can be found at `http://wordpressphonegap.liangeugene.com`. If you've got any questions, feel free to visit.

Index

Thank you for buying
WordPress Mobile Applications with PhoneGap

About Packt Publishing

Packt, pronounced 'packed', published its first book "*Mastering phpMyAdmin for Effective MySQL Management*" in April 2004 and subsequently continued to specialize in publishing highly focused books on specific technologies and solutions.

Our books and publications share the experiences of your fellow IT professionals in adapting and customizing today's systems, applications, and frameworks. Our solution based books give you the knowledge and power to customize the software and technologies you're using to get the job done. Packt books are more specific and less general than the IT books you have seen in the past. Our unique business model allows us to bring you more focused information, giving you more of what you need to know, and less of what you don't.

Packt is a modern, yet unique publishing company, which focuses on producing quality, cutting-edge books for communities of developers, administrators, and newbies alike. For more information, please visit our website: www.packtpub.com.

About Packt Open Source

In 2010, Packt launched two new brands, Packt Open Source and Packt Enterprise, in order to continue its focus on specialization. This book is part of the Packt Open Source brand, home to books published on software built around Open Source licences, and offering information to anybody from advanced developers to budding web designers. The Open Source brand also runs Packt's Open Source Royalty Scheme, by which Packt gives a royalty to each Open Source project about whose software a book is sold.

Writing for Packt

We welcome all inquiries from people who are interested in authoring. Book proposals should be sent to author@packtpub.com. If your book idea is still at an early stage and you would like to discuss it first before writing a formal book proposal, contact us; one of our commissioning editors will get in touch with you.

We're not just looking for published authors; if you have strong technical skills but no writing experience, our experienced editors can help you develop a writing career, or simply get some additional reward for your expertise.

PhoneGap Beginner's Guide

ISBN: 978-1-84951-536-8   Paperback: 328 pages

Build cross-platform mobile applications with the
PhoneGap open source development framework

1. Learn how to use the PhoneGap mobile
    application framework

2. Develop cross-platform code for iOS, Android,
    BlackBerry, and more

3. Write robust and extensible JavaScript code

4. Master new HTML5 and CSS3 APIs

jQuery Mobile Web Development Essentials

ISBN: 978-1-84951-726-3   Paperback: 246 pages

Learn to use the touch-optimized, cross-device,
cross-platform jQM web framework for smartphones
and tablets

1. Create websites that work beautifully on a wide
    range of mobile devices with jQuery mobile

2. Learn to prepare your jQuery mobile project by
    learning through three sample applications

3. Packed with easy to follow examples and clear
    explanations of how to easily build mobile-
    optimized websites

Please check **www.PacktPub.com** for information on our titles

jQuery Mobile First Look

ISBN: 978-1-84951-590-0   Paperback: 216 pages

Discover the endless possibilities offered by jQuery Mobile for rapid mobile web development

1. Easily create your mobile web applications from scratch with jQuery Mobile

2. Learn the important elements of the framework and mobile web development best practices

3. Customize elements and widgets to match your desired style

4. Step-by-step instructions on how to use jQuery Mobile

jQuery Mobile Cookbook

ISBN: 978-1-84951-722-5   Paperback: 320 pages

Over 80 recipes with examples and practical tips to help you quickly learn and develop cross-platform applications with jQuery Mobile

1. Create applications that use custom animations and use various techniques to improve application performance

2. Use and customize the various controls such as toolbars, buttons, and lists with custom icons, icon sprites, styles, and themes

3. Write simple but powerful scripts to manipulate the various configurations and work with the events, methods, and utilities which are provided by the framework

Please check **www.PacktPub.com** for information on our titles

www.ingramcontent.com/pod-product-compliance
Lightning Source LLC
LaVergne TN
LVHW080102070326
832902LV00014B/2376